FOOTBALL SUPERSTARS ALBUM 1993

RICHARD J. BRENNER

16 FULL-PAGE SUPERSTAR POSTERS

TEAM AND INDIVIDUAL STATS

East End Publishing, Ltd.
Syosset, NY

Author's Note: All of the players in this book are gifted athletes. But they all had to work hard and overcome obstacles to achieve their success.

You can become a superstar, too, if you want to work for it. And there are lots of areas for you to consider besides athletics. You can help clean up the earth or work for world peace. You can become a musician or a teacher. The planet needs superstar ecologists and care givers even more than it needs superstar athletes.

Mr. Brenner is the noted author of many other sports books including BASKETBALL SUPERSTARS ALBUM 1993, FOOTBALL SUPERSTARS ALBUM 1993, BASEBALL SUPERSTARS ALBUM 1993, THE COMPLETE SUPER BOWL STORY I–XXVII and THE WORLD SERIES, THE GREAT CONTESTS; DUAL BIOGRAPHIES OF SHAQUILLE O'NEAL & LARRY JOHNSON and JOE MONTANA & JERRY RICE; and, now, there is a new series of easy-to-read photo-filled biographies on Michael Jordan, Wayne Gretzky and Macaulay Culkin.

For complete details on how to order these and other exciting sports books, please see back page.

Mr. Brenner is also available to speak to student groups. For details contact East End Publishing, Ltd. 54 Alexander Drive, Syosset, NY 11791, (516) 364-6383.

To Jason, Halle and Anita, with love. Thanks for your encouragement, enthusiasm, and help.

Photo Credits: The cover photo of Troy Aikman was taken by Robert Tringali, Jr. and supplied by SPORTSCHROME EAST/WEST. SPORTSCHROME also supplied the following photographs: Warren Moon, Eric Allen and John Elway by Robert Tringali, Jr.; and Dan Marino by Rich Kane. Cortez Kennedy was photographed by Dave Gaddis. All other photos were supplied by ALLSPORT USA, as per the following: Junior Seau by Stephen Dunn; Sam Mills and Emmitt Smith by Mike Powell; Michael Irvin and Jerry Rice by Otto Greule, Jr.; Barry Foster, Deion Sanders, Thurman Thomas and Jim Kelly by Rick Stewart; Barry Sanders by Jonathan Daniel; and Steve Young by Jim Commentucci.

ISBN 0-943403-21-9 Cover design by Stephen Bell

Printed in the United States of America

FINAL 1992 STANDINGS

National Conference

Eastern Division

Team	W	L	T	Pct	PF	PA	Home	Away	AFC	NFC	Div
Dallas	13	3	0	.813	409	243	7-1-0	6-2-0	4-0-0	9-3-0	6-2-0
Philadelphia	11	5	0	.688	354	245	8-0-0	3-5-0	3-1-0	8-4-0	6-2-0
Washington	9	7	0	.563	300	255	6-2-0	3-5-0	2-2-0	7-5-0	4-4-0
Giants	6	10	0	.375	306	367	4-4-0	2-6-0	2-2-0	4-8-0	2-6-0
Phoenix	4	12	0	.250	243	332	3-5-0	1-7-0	0-2-0	4-10-0	2-6-0

Central Division

Team	W	L	T	Pct	PF	PA	Home	Away	AFC	NFC	Div
Minnesota	11	5	0	.688	374	249	5-3-0	6-2-0	3-1-0	8-4-0	7-1-0
Green Bay	9	7	0	.563	276	296	6-2-0	3-5-0	3-1-0	6-6-0	4-4-0
Tampa Bay	5	11	0	.313	267	365	3-5-0	2-6-0	0-2-0	5-9-0	3-5-0
Chicago	5	11	0	.313	295	361	4-4-0	1-7-0	1-3-0	4-8-0	3-5-0
Detroit	5	11	0	.313	273	332	3-5-0	2-6-0	2-2-0	3-9-0	3-5-0

Western Division

Team	W	L	T	Pct	PF	PA	Home	Away	AFC	NFC	Div
San Francisco	14	2	0	.875	431	236	7-1-0	7-1-0	3-1-0	11-1-0	6-0-0
New Orleans	12	4	0	.750	330	202	6-2-0	6-2-0	3-1-0	9-3-0	4-2-0
Atlanta	6	10	0	.375	327	414	5-3-0	1-7-0	2-2-0	4-8-0	1-5-0
L.A. Rams	6	10	0	.375	313	383	4-4-0	2-6-0	2-2-0	4-8-0	1-5-0

American Conference

Eastern Division

Team	W	L	T	Pct	PF	PA	Home	Away	AFC	NFC	Div
Miami	11	5	0	.688	340	281	6-2-0	5-3-0	9-3-0	2-2-0	5-3-0
Buffalo	11	5	0	.688	381	283	6-2-0	5-3-0	7-5-0	4-0-0	5-3-0
Indianapolis	9	7	0	.563	216	302	4-4-0	5-3-0	7-7-0	2-0-0	5-3-0
Jets	4	12	0	.250	220	315	3-5-0	1-7-0	4-8-0	0-4-0	3-5-0
New England	2	14	0	.125	205	363	1-7-0	1-7-0	2-10-0	0-4-0	2-6-0

Central Division

Team	W	L	T	Pct	PF	PA	Home	Away	AFC	NFC	Div
Pittsburgh	11	5	0	.688	299	225	7-1-0	4-4-0	10-2-0	1-3-0	5-1-0
Houston	10	6	0	.625	352	258	5-3-0	5-3-0	7-5-0	3-1-0	5-1-0
Cleveland	7	9	0	.438	272	275	4-4-0	3-5-0	5-7-0	2-2-0	3-3-0
Cincinnati	5	11	0	.313	274	364	3-5-0	2-6-0	4-8-0	1-3-0	1-5-0

Western Division

Team	W	L	T	Pct	PF	PA	Home	Away	AFC	NFC	Div
San Diego	11	5	0	.688	335	241	6-2-0	5-3-0	9-5-0	2-0-0	5-3-0
Kansas City	10	6	0	.625	348	282	7-1-0	3-5-0	8-4-0	2-2-0	6-2-0
Denver	8	8	0	.500	262	329	7-1-0	1-7-0	7-5-0	1-3-0	1-3-0
L.A. Raiders	7	9	0	.438	249	329	5-3-0	2-6-0	5-7-0	2-2-0	4-4-0
Seattle	2	14	0	.125	140	312	1-7-0	1-7-0	2-10-0	0-4-0	1-7-0

1992 NFL POSTSEASON AT A GLANCE

(Attendance in parenthesis; home team in caps)

AFC Wild Card Playoff Games
SAN DIEGO 17, Kansas City 0 (58,278)
BUFFALO 41, Houston 38 (OT) (75,141)

AFC Divisional Playoff Games
Buffalo 24, PITTSBURGH 3 (60,407)
MIAMI 31, San Diego 0 (71,224)

AFC Championship Game
Buffalo 29, MIAMI 10 (72,703)

NFC Wild Card Playoff Games
Washington 24, MINNESOTA 7 (57,353)
Philadelphia 36, NEW ORLEANS 20 (68,591)

NFC Divisional Playoff Games
SAN FRANCISCO 20, Washington 13 (64,991)
DALLAS 34, Philadelphia 10 (63,721)

NFC Championship Game
Dallas 30, SAN FRANCISCO 20 (65,019)

Super Bowl XXVII at Rose Bowl, Pasadena, California
DALLAS 52, Buffalo 17 (98,374)

AFC–NFC Pro Bowl at Aloha Stadium, Honolulu, Hawaii
AFC 23, NFC 20 (50,007)

N.F.C. LEADERS

QUARTERBACKS

	Att	Comp	Pct Comp	Yds	Avg Gain	TD	Int	Rating Points
Young, Steve, S.F.	402	268	66.7	3465	8.62	25	7	107.0
Miller, Chris, Atl.	253	152	60.1	1739	6.87	15	6	90.7
Aikman, Troy, Dal.	473	302	63.8	3445	7.28	23	14	89.5
Cunningham, Randall, Phi.	384	233	60.7	2775	7.23	19	11	87.3
Favre, Brett, G.B.	471	302	64.1	3227	6.85	18	13	85.3
Hebert, Bobby, N.O.	422	249	59.0	3287	7.79	19	16	82.9
Everett, Jim, Rams	475	281	59.2	3323	7.00	22	18	80.2
Chandler, Chris, Pho.	413	245	59.3	2832	6.86	15	15	77.1
Harbaugh, Jim, Chi.	358	202	56.4	2486	6.94	13	12	76.2
Testaverde, Vinny, T.B.	358	206	57.5	2554	7.13	14	16	74.2
Gannon, Rich, Min	279	159	57.0	1905	6.83	12	13	72.9
Rypien, Mark, Was.	479	269	56.2	3282	6.85	13	17	71.7

RUSHERS

	Att	Yards	Avg	Long	TD
Smith, Emmitt, Dal.	373	1713	4.6	68t	18
Sanders, Barry, Det.	312	1352	4.3	55t	9
Allen, Terry, Min.	266	1201	4.5	51	13
Cobb, Reggie, T.B.	310	1171	3.8	25	9
Hampton, Rodney, NY-G.	257	1141	4.4	63t	14
Gary, Cleveland, Rams	279	1125	4.0	63	7
Walker, Herschel, Phi.	267	1070	4.0	38	8
Watters, Ricky, S.F.	206	1013	4.9	43	9
Byner, Earnest, Was.	262	998	3.8	23	6
Johnson, Johnny, Pho.	178	734	4.1	42t	6
Workman, Vince, G.B.	159	631	4.0	44	2
Sherman, Heath, Phi.	112	583	5.2	34	5
Anderson, Neal, Chi.	156	582	3.7	49t	5

RECEIVERS

	No	Yards	Avg	Long	TD
Sharpe, Sterling, G.B.	108	1461	13.5	76t	13
Rison, Andre, Atl.	93	1119	12.0	71t	11
Rice, Jerry, S.F.	84	1201	14.3	80t	10
Irvin, Michael, Dal.	78	1396	17.9	87t	7
Pritchard, Mike, Atl.	77	827	10.7	38t	5
Perriman, Brett, Det.	69	810	11.7	40t	4
Martin, Eric, N.O.	68	1041	15.3	52t	5
Novacek, Jay, Dal.	68	630	9.3	34	6
Barnett, Fred, Phi.	67	1083	16.2	71t	6
Clark, Gary, Was.	64	776	12.9	41	1
Dawsey, Lawrence, T.B.	60	776	12.9	41	1
Proehl, Ricky, Pho.	60	744	12.4	63t	3
Hill, Drew, Atl.	60	623	10.4	43	3

PUNTERS

	No	Yards	Avg	Long	Total Punts
Newsome, Harry, Min.	72	3243	45.0	84	73
Barnhardt, Tommy, N.O.	67	2947	44.0	62	67
Arnold, Jim, Det.	65	2846	43.8	71	66
Landeta, Sean, NY-G	53	2317	43.7	71	55
Saxon, Mike, Dal.	61	2620	43.0	58	61
Gardocki, Chris, Chi.	79	3393	42.9	61	79
Camarillo, Rich, Pho.	54	2317	42.9	73	54
Feagles, Jeff, Phi.	82	3459	42.2	68	82
Rodriguez, Ruben, Den.-NY-G	46	1907	41.5	55	47
Fulhage, Scott, Atl.	68	2818	41.4	56	69
Bracken, Don, Rams	76	3122	41.1	59	76
Stryzinski, Dan, T.B.	74	3015	40.7	57	74

PUNT RETURNERS

	No	FC	Yards	Avg	Long	TD
Bailey, Johnny, Pho.	20	8	263	13.2	65	0
Martin, Kelvin, Dal.	42	18	532	12.7	79t	2
Sikahema, Vai, Phi.	40	10	503	12.6	87t	1
Parker, Anthony, Min.	33	17	336	10.2	42	0
Buckley, Terrell, G.B.	21	5	211	10.0	58t	1
Mitchell, Brian, Was.	29	9	271	9.3	84t	1
Meggett, Dave, NY-G	27	11	240	8.9	39	0
Grant, Alan, S.F.	29	10	249	8.6	46	0
Turner, Vernon, Rams	28	6	207	7.4	23	0
Newman, Pat, N.O.	23	10	158	6.9	18	0

KICKOFF RETURNERS

	No	Yards	Avg	Long	TD
Sanders, Deion, Atl.	40	1067	26.7	99t	2
Bailey, Johnny, Pho.	28	690	24.6	63	0
Gray, Mel, Det.	f42	1006	24.0	89t	1
Meggett, Dave, NY-G	20	455	22.8	92t	1
Lewis, Darren, Chi.	23	511	22.2	97t	1
Logan, Marc, S.F.	22	478	21.7	82	0
Nelson, Darrin, Min.	29	626	21.6	53	0
Mitchell, Brian, Was.	23	492	21.4	47	0
Howard, Desmond, Was.	22	462	21.0	42	0
Martin, Kelvin, Dal.	24	503	21.0	59	0
Harris, Corey, Hou.-G.B.	33	691	20.9	50	0
Sikahema, Vai, Phi.	26	528	20.3	41	0

TOUCHDOWN LEADERS

	TD	Rush	Rec	Misc.	Pts
Smith, Emmitt, Dal.	19	18	1	0	114
Allen, Terry, Min.	15	13	2	0	90
Hampton, Rodney, NY-G	14	14	0	0	84
Sharpe, Sterling, G.B.	13	0	13	0	78
Anderson, Neal, Chi.	11	5	6	0	66
Rice, Jerry, S.F.	11	1	10	0	66
Rison, Andre, Atl.	11	0	11	0	66
Watters, Ricky, S.F.	11	9	2	0	66
Gary, Cleveland, Rams	10	7	3	0	60
Haynes, Michael, Atl.	10	0	10	0	60
Sanders, Barry, Det.	10	9	1	0	60
Walker, Herschel, Phi.	10	8	2	0	60
Cobb, Reggie, T.B.	9	9	0	0	54

KICKING

	EP	EPA	FG	FGA	PTS
Andersen, Morten, N.O.	33	34	29	34	120
Lohmiller, Chip, Was.	30	30	30	40	120
Elliott, Lin, Dal.	47	48	24	35	119
Cofer, Mike, S.F.	53	54	18	27	107
Reveiz, Fuad, Min.	45	45	19	25	102
Jacke, Chris, G.B.	30	30	22	29	96
Hanson, Jason, Det.	30	30	21	26	93
Johnson, Norm, Atl.	39	39	18	22	93
Butler, Kevin, Chi.	34	34	19	26	91
Ruzek, Roger, Phi.	40	44	16	25	88
Zendejas, Tony, Rams	38	38	15	20	83

TEAM OFFENSE

	Rush Yds.	Pass Yds.	Tot. Yds.	Rush TD	Pass TD	Misc. TD	E.P.	F.G./F.G.A.	Points
San Francisco	2315	3880	6195	22	29	3	53	18/27	431
Dallas	2121	3485	5606	20	23	5	47	24/35	409
Minnesota	2030	2869	4899	19	18	8	45	19/25	374
Philadelphia	2388	2592	4980	19	20	5	40	16/25	354
New Orleans	1628	3178	4806	10	19	6	33	29/34	330
Atlanta	1270	3633	4903	3	33	3	39	18/22	327
L.A. Rams	1659	3218	4877	12	23	3	38	15/20	313
N.Y. Giants	2077	2345	4422	20	14	2	36	18/23	306
Washington	1727	3163	4890	10	15	5	30	30/40	300
Chicago	1871	3070	4941	15	17	2	34	19/26	295
Green Bay	1555	3230	4785	7	20	3	30	22/29	276
Detroit	1644	2796	4440	9	16	5	30	21/26	273
Tampa Bay	1706	3065	4771	12	17	4	33	12/22	267
Phoenix	1491	3086	4577	11	15	3	28	13/26	243

SACK LEADERS

Simmons, Clyde, Phi.	19.0
Harris, Tim, S.F.	17.0
Martin, Wayne, N.O.	15.5
Doleman, Chris, Min.	14.5
White, Reggie, Phi.	14.0
Bennett, Tony, G.B.	13.5
Jackson, Rickey, N.O.	13.5
Randle, John, Min.	11.5
Jeffcoat, Jim, Dal.	10.5
McMichael, Steve, Chi.	10.5
Swilling, Pat, N.O.	10.5
Dotson, Santana, T.B.	10.0
Greene, Kevin, Rams	10.0

INTERCEPTION LEADERS

	No	Yards	Avg	Long	TD
McMillian, Audray, Min.	8	157	19.6	51t	2
Woolford, Donnell, Chi.	7	67	9.6	32	0
Edwards, Brad, Was.	6	157	26.2	53t	1
Cook, Toi, N.O.	6	90	15.0	48t	1
Massey, Robert, Pho.	5	147	29.4	46t	3
Scott, Todd, Min.	5	79	15.8	35t	1
Glenn, Vencie, Min.	5	65	13.0	39	0
Griffin, Don, S.F.	5	4	0.8	2	0
Joyner, Seth, Phi.	4	88	22.0	43t	2
Evans, Byron, Phi.	4	76	19.0	43	0

TEAM DEFENSE

	Rush Yds.	Pass Yds.	Tot. Yds.	Opp. TD	Rush TD	Pass TD	Ret. TD	Sacks	Int.	Pts. Allow
New Orleans	1605	2470	4075	24	8	13	3	57	18	202
San Francisco	1418	3369	4787	27	5	20	2	41	17	236
Dallas	1244	2687	3931	29	11	16	2	44	17	243
Philadelphia	1481	2931	4412	26	4	20	2	55	24	245
Minnesota	1733	2782	4515	27	11	12	4	51	28	249
Washington	1696	2742	4438	30	11	15	4	39	23	255
Green Bay	1821	3277	5098	32	12	16	4	34	15	296
Detroit	1841	3217	5058	38	14	20	4	29	21	332
Phoenix	1635	3491	5126	40	13	24	3	27	16	332
Chicago	1948	3004	4952	43	14	20	9	43	14	361
Tampa Bay	1675	3510	5185	43	15	25	3	36	20	365
NY Giants	2012	3031	5043	46	17	22	7	25	14	367
LA Rams	2230	3293	5523	43	22	18	3	31	18	383
Atlanta	2294	3255	5549	51	20	24	7	31	11	414

PRO BOWL ROSTER
NATIONAL CONFERENCE

OFFENSE

WIDE RECEIVERS—Jerry Rice, 49ers; Andre Rison, Falcons; Sterling Sharpe, Packers; Fred Barnett, Eagles; Michael Irvin, Cowboys.
TIGHT ENDS—Brent Jones, 49ers; Jay Novacek, Cowboys.
TACKLES—Gary Zimmerman, Vikings; Steve Wallace, 49ers; Lomas Brown, Lions.
GUARDS—Nate Newton, Cowboys; Guy McIntyre, 49ers; Randall McDaniel, Vikings.
CENTERS—Mark Stepnoski, Cowboys; Joel, Hilgenberg, Saints.
QUARTERBACKS—Brett Favre, Packers; Steve Young, 49ers; Troy Aikman, Cowboys.
RUNNING BACKS—Barry Sanders, Lions; Emmitt Smith, Cowboys; Rodney Hampton, Giants; Ricky Watters, 49ers.

DEFENSE

DEFENSIVE ENDS—Chris Doleman, Vikings; Reggie White, Eagles; Clyde Simmons, Eagles.
NOSE TACKLES—Pierce Holt, 49ers; Henry Thomas, Vikings.
LINEBACKERS—Mike Singletary, Bears; Sam Mills, Saints; Vaughan Johnson, Saints; Patt Swilling, Saints; Rickey Jackson, Saints; Wilber Marshall, Redskins; Jessie Tuggle, Falcons.
CORNERBACKS—Eric Allen, Eagles; Deion Sanders, Falcons; Robert Massey, Cardinals.
SAFETIES—Chuck Cecil, Packers; Todd Scott, Vikings; Tim McDonald, Cardinals.

SPECIALISTS

PUNTER—Rich Camarillo, Cardinals.

PLACE-KICKER—Morten Andersen, Saints.

KICK RETURNER—Johnny Bailey, Cardinals.

SPECIAL TEAMS—Elbert Shelley, Falcons.

JERRY RICE

WIDE RECEIVER

SAN FRANCISCO 49ERS

JERRY RICE
SAN FRANCISCO 49ERS

After eight record-shattering seasons, Jerry Rice has removed all doubt about who rules the roost when it comes to wide receivers. "I've seen them all," said Steve Sabol, the president of NFL Films, "and Rice is the greatest receiver to ever play the game."

Rice started terrorizing defensive secondaries at his first training camp. "He intimidated many of our defensive backs, to a point where they started off the season without any confidence," recalled 49ers coach George Seifert.

Once the season started, though, Rice had trouble holding on to the football and was even benched for a short time. "But I didn't lose my confidence, I just worked harder," said Rice. "I learned at an early age that I had to work hard to achieve anything in this life." And the extra effort paid off in the 14th week of the season when Rice broke out in a big way against the Los Angeles Rams, catching 10 passes for a team-record 241 yards. "That was my coming-out game," said Rice, who has gone on to turn his career into a non-stop highlight tape.

In his second season, Rice piled up 1,570 receiving yards, the third highest total that had ever been recorded in the NFL, scored 15 touchdowns, and was named the Player of the Year by *Sports Illustrated.* "Jerry became so good so fast, it scares you sometimes," said Dennis Green, who was the 49ers receiving coach. "He just explodes toward the ball. If a pass is near him, it's his."

The following year, Rice was named the NFL's MVP when he did the unimaginable by hauling in a record-shattering 22 touchdown receptions in a 12-game strike-shortened season. And one year later Rice topped off his third consecutive All-Pro season by snaring 21 passes for a record-tying six touchdowns in three postseason games. Included in Rice's rampage was a record-setting 215-yard performance against Cincinnati which earned him the MVP trophy in Super Bowl XXIII.

"Jerry Rice is in another world," said an awed Bengals defender, David Fulcher.

Although NFL defensive backs might have preferred to see Rice on another planet, he remained on earth and led all NFL receivers in yardage gained and touchdowns scored during the 1989 season. Then he tacked on another five scores in postseason play, including a record-setting three-touchdown-reception effort in Super Bowl XXIV.

Rice had another remarkable season in 1990, tying an NFL record with five scoring receptions in a game against Atlanta, while once again leading the league in receiving yardage and receptions and becoming only the fourth player in NFL history to catch 100 passes in a single season. "When I'm running down the field and the ball is in the air, I don't hear anything. No footsteps, no crowd, nothing. It's like I'm in a trance, just me and the ball."

Rice, who has caught at least one pass in 111 consecutive games while going over the 1,000-yard receiving mark in seven straight seasons, continued his unswerving assault on the NFL record book in 1992 by becoming the career leader in touchdown receptions with 103. And then Rice gave NFL defensive backs a nightmarish thought to ponder in the offseason. "I feel like I'm still getting better. I feel like I could play another 10 seasons or so."

Born: October 13, 1962, in Starkville, Mississippi
Height: 6′2″ Weight: 200
College: Mississippi Valley State
Round Drafted: First
NFL Seasons Played: 8

CAREER STATS

RECEPTS.	*YDS.*	*AVG.*	*TD'S*
610	10,273	16.8	103

DEION SANDERS

DEFENSIVE BACK

ATLANTA FALCONS

DEION SANDERS
ATLANTA FALCONS

Deion Sanders has been a prime-time performer since he was an 8-year-old playing Little League baseball and Pop Warner football. "And I have the films to prove it," said Sanders. "I've been in the spotlight at every level. It's just a bigger spotlight now."

Sanders was a three-sport star at North Fort Myers High School in Florida, where he was an all-state basketball player, who averaged 24 points a game in his senior season, and earned his nickname, *"Prime Time."* "A buddy named me that after I dunked over everybody for 30 points in one game." He was also an all-state baseball player who showed enough potential to be offered a minor league contract by the Kansas City Royals. But Deion instead chose to accept a football scholarship to Florida State University.

Sanders became a four-year starter and an expert trash talker at FSU. One time he told a receiver, "We're out in front of 60,000 people in the Orange Bowl, and you run this ugly pass pattern that I have to follow. Man, that's embarrassing to the both of us." But Deion, who never talks meanly or curses, backed up his words with deeds, as he became a two-time All-American, and in his senior season led the nation's punt returners with a 15.2-yard average and won the Jim Thorpe Award as the top defensive back in college football.

After Sanders was snatched up by the Falcons in the 1989 draft, he introduced himself to his new fans. "Hello Atlanta. This is Deion Sanders. Prime Time. Live. It's five minutes to eight, and the thrill is here. Later."

And five minutes into his first NFL game, Sanders brought Atlanta fans out of their seats by turning a punt return into a 68-yard touchdown excursion. "In 27 years in this league, I've never experienced the buzz that goes through a stadium when this guy gets near the ball," said Marion Campbell, Atlanta's head coach during Sanders' rookie season. "This guy is a great defensive back," said CBS sportscaster John Madden. "He's a superstar."

Sanders, who is one of the fastest runners in the NFL, quickly established himself as one of the league's top return specialists while also becoming one of the NFL's very best cornerbacks. "I tried to throw a spin move on him," said 49ers running back Rickey Watters, "but he caught me halfway between my spin. He came at me so fast, I felt like I was in a cartoon or something."

Prime Time continued to make it show time in 1992, by leading the league in kickoff return average, and topping the Pro Bowl balloting at two positions—cornerback and kick returner. "He's the greatest athlete I've ever seen," said Ken Herock, the Falcons' director of player personnel. "Deion can play wide receiver [which he has done a few times]; he could play tailback. He can do anything."

Sanders has also been doubling up as a major league baseball player, first with the New York Yankees, and, since 1991, with the Atlanta Braves. Although Sanders' baseball career got off to a slow start, he seemed to hit his stride in 1992, as he used his sprinter's speed to stroke a major-league-high 14 triples while batting .304. Sanders' star shined even brighter in the 1992 World Series, as he topped all hitters with a .533 batting average. "He's a tremendous baseball player," said Braves general manager John Schuerholz. "You can see the excitement and energy level of the club rise when he plays."

Although Sanders has sent conflicting signals as to whether he'll continue to play both sports, whatever he does, he'll be doing it in Prime Time style. Live and with thrills.

Born: August 9, 1967, in Fort Myers, Florida
Height: 6′0″ Weight: 185
College: Florida State University
Round Drafted: First
NFL Seasons Played: 4

CAREER STATS

		RET. YDS. AVG.		
INT.	*YDS.*	*PUNTS*	*KICKOFFS*	*TD'S*
17	429	8.4	23.0	9

SAM MILLS

LINEBACKER

NEW ORLEANS SAINTS

SAM MILLS
NEW ORLEANS SAINTS

Sam Mills has taken a long and winding road to NFL stardom. And although he needed a jump-start from a friendly coach, once he set out on his journey, Mills didn't allow obstacles or disappointments to block his way.

Mills started his football career in New Jersey, where Frank Glazier, the Long Beach High School coach, taught him the basic linebacking techniques that Mills is still using today. "He taught me how to read keys and how to square my shoulders up with the line of scrimmage to take on a block and deliver a blow. He taught me the basics and I just built from there." Glazier also encouraged Mills, who was expecting to finish high school and become an auto mechanic, to instead go on to college. When Mills balked, Glazier simply switched Mills' classes, and signed him up into a college prep program. "He never gave me the chance to refuse," said Mills. "He changed my life."

Mills didn't win a scholarship, or go to a school with a big-time college football program. But he did get an education at Montclair State in New Jersey, and he also went on to become the football team's captain and earn Division II All-American honors as a senior, while being named the 1980 All-East Defensive Player of the Year.

After Mills, who had gone undrafted by any NFL team, failed free agent tryouts, first with the Cleveland Browns and then with the Toronto Argonauts of the Canadian Football League, he went home to New Jersey and began teaching. But when a new football league started operations a few months later, Mills decided to resign his teaching position and try out for one of the new United States Football League teams, the Philadelphia Stars. "It was a chance I had to take, because I felt that, given the right opportunity, I could stick with a team."

And once he got his foot in the door, he never took it out. "You talk about someone who was psyched up and ready to play. When I took the field for the first game I had tears in my eyes. I felt like I hadn't really made the team yet, and that if I had a bad day I'd be gone," said Mills, who went on to play every down over three straight seasons for the Stars while helping to lead them to two USFL titles.

When the USFL folded following the 1986 season, Mills showed that he had become a prime-time player by earning a starting spot with the New Orleans Saints. Mills has gone on to become one of the best inside linebackers in the NFL, earning four trips to the Pro Bowl and becoming the leader of one of the league's top defenses.

"Nobody gets more out of his ability than Sam Mills," said Saints head coach Jim Mora. "He's the best football player I've ever been around."

Born: June 3, 1959, in Neptune, New Jersey
Height: 5′9″ Weight: 225
College: Montclair State
Round Drafted: Signed as a free agent
NFL Seasons Played: 7

CAREER STATS

		FUMBLES		
TACKLES	*SACKS*	*FORCED*	*RECOVERED*	*INT.*
694	7.5	12	15	3

MICHAEL IRVIN

WIDE RECEIVER

DALLAS COWBOYS

MICHAEL IRVIN
DALLAS COWBOYS

Micahel Irvin, who grew up with 16 sisters and brothers, was always hungry. "In my family, when you sat down to eat, you ate all you could, because you didn't know when you'd eat again."

Irvin takes that same attitude out to the football field, where he devours defensive backs as if each one might be his last meal. "I have to put everything into each play, because any play could be my last play."

At the University of Miami, where he became a three-year starter, and set career records for catches (143), receiving yards (2,423), and touchdown receptions (26), Irvin showed why his teammates had nicknamed him The Playmaker when, in his senior season, he keyed the Hurricanes' run to the 1987 national championship.

First, Irvin knocked cross-state rival Florida State University from the ranks of the undefeated by snaring two fourth-quarter touchdown grabs against a defensive backfield that featured All-American Deion Sanders. Then Irvin came up with the game-winning touchdown in Miami's Orange Bowl win over Oklahoma that locked up the No. 1 ranking for the 'Canes.

When the Cowboys lassoed Irvin with the 11th pick of the 1988 NFL draft, Tex Schramm, the Dallas general manager at the time, declared, "This accelerates our rise to the living."

Irvin showed signs of future stardom in his rookie year by averaging an NFC-best 20.4 yards per catch. Then, after two injury-plagued seasons had slowed his progress, Irvin burst forth as a full-fledged superstar in 1991. The Playmaker produced one of the greatest seasons ever posted by a wide receiver, as he compiled a league-leading 1,523 receiving yards, the sixth highest total in NFL history, and pulled down 93 passes, the seventh highest total ever recorded.

Irvin's most significant catches were made while Dallas was running off a season-ending five-game winning streak that catapulted the Cowboys into the playoffs for the first time since 1985. During the stretch run, Irvin caught 37 passes, covering 649 yards and four touchdowns, and he caught them against the league's leading cornerbacks, including Washington's Darrell Green, Pittsburgh's Rod Woodson, Philadelphia's Eric Allen, and Atlanta's Deion Sanders. "Those are the games I enjoy. That's when you take it to another level," said the Playmaker. "I'm coming to catch the ball and I don't care who you have back there."

The always-hungry Irvin, who had made the All-Pro team and been named the NFL Alumni Wide Receiver of the Year, worked harder than ever preparing for his next season. "I've got to get better. I feel that if I'm sitting still, somebody is catching up to me."

Then Irvin showed he wasn't a one-trick pony by turning in an almost carbon-copy season in 1992, which he capped off with a Super Bowl spectacular that included six catches for 114 yards and two second quarter touchdowns, 18 seconds apart, that turned the tide in Dallas' favor.

"You'll never hear me say that I'm the best receiver who ever played the game," said the 49ers' Jerry Rice, who is generally considered to be the top pass catcher of all-time. "I'll give that to Michael. Michael is the Playmaker, the best in the game."

And still hungry.

Born: March 5, 1966, in Ft. Lauderdale, Florida
Height: 6′2″ Weight: 199
College: University of Miami
Round Drafted: First
NFL Seasons Played: 5

CAREER STATS

RECEPTS.	*YDS.*	*AVG.*	*TD'S*
249	4,364	17.5	27

BARRY SANDERS

RUNNING BACK
DETROIT LIONS

BARRY SANDERS
DETROIT LIONS

Barry Sanders is the most elusive and electrifying runner in the NFL. "The guy is so good that he not only picks up his yards, but he makes defenses look foolish in the process," said Miami nose tackle Shawn Lee. "But what else can you look like when you reach out to grab him and all you get is air?"

No one, however, looks more foolish than the coach at North High School in Wichita, Kansas who kept Sanders out of the offensive backfield until the sixth game of his senior season. With his sprinter's speed and amazing moves, Sanders showed why he belonged by rushing for 274 yards and four touchdowns in his first game as a running back. And even with his late start, Sanders went on to set the city's single-season rushing record by racking up 1,417 yards.

But even after Sanders had turned in such a spectacular season, most college scouts were turned off by his lack of size. "It's amazing to me how much attention coaches and scouts pay to size, instead of talent," said Sanders. "The fact that most of the big schools ignored me didn't discourage me, though. It gave me incentive to show them it's not all about size."

Sanders did receive a scholarship to Oklahoma State University, but he spent his first two seasons playing second fiddle to Thurman Thomas, the All-Pro back of the Buffalo Bills, who was closing out his All-American college career at OSU. But Sanders did get a lot of playing time on the special teams, and did so in spectacular style in his sophomore season by leading the nation in kickoff returns while finishing second in punt returns. Sanders also spent a lot of time in OSU's weight room, building up his legs so that he'd be ready to carry the load when his time came.

In his junior year, with Thomas graduated, Sanders became the featured back in the Cowboys' attack, and all he did was put together one of the greatest single-season performances in college football history. With a display of running that left defenders defenseless, Sanders set 13 NCAA records, including most rushing yards (2,628) and touchdowns scored (39) in a season, on his way to winning the 1988 Heisman Trophy as the best college player in the country.

Sanders has gone on to attain that same level of success in the NFL, where he has gained more yards rushing (5674) and scored more rushing touchdowns (52) than any other player during the past four seasons. "He makes you stand on your toes every time he gets the ball," said Detroit Lions coach Wayne Fontes. "You watch because you feel like something big's about to happen."

Born: July 16, 1968, in Wichita, Kansas
Height: 5′8″ Weight: 203
College: Oklahoma Sate University
Round Drafted: First
NFL Seasons Played: 4

CAREER STATS

RUSH		*RECEPTS.*		
YDS.	*AVG.*	*NO.*	*YDS.*	*TD'S*
5,674	4.8	129	1,276	57

STEVE YOUNG

QUARTERBACK

SAN FRANCISCO 49ERS

STEVE YOUNG
SAN FRANCISCO 49ERS

Steve Young has taken a long, strange trip, indeed, to become the star quarterback of the San Francisco 49ers.

After a brilliant senior season at Brigham Young University, in which he threw for 3,902 yards and 33 touchdowns, while completing a record-setting 71.3 percent of his passes, Young decided to sidestep the NFL entirely and sign a 40-million-dollar contract with the Los Angeles Express of the fledgling United States Football League.

Young spent two seasons with the Express, during which he became the first pro quarterback to rush for 100 yards and pass for 300 yards in a single game. Then, after the USFL folded in 1985, Young signed with Tampa Bay, but after two mediocre seasons with the Buccaneers he was traded to San Francisco as a backup to Joe Montana, the 49ers' All-Pro signal caller.

Young saw only limited action during his first four seasons in San Francisco, while Montana guided the 49ers to two Super Bowl championships and solidified his reputation as one of the greatest quarterbacks of all time. And when Young did finally get a chance to strut his stuff in 1991, while Montana was sidelined with a season-long elbow injury, he produced only mixed results. Although Young did wind up at the top of the league's statistical rankings, the team struggled to a 5–5 standstill in his 10 starts. That record stood in stark contrast to the 5–1 mark turned in by Steve Bono, who had taken over the quarterbacking reigns after Young had gone down with a knee injury. So when the 49ers failed to make the playoffs for the first time in 10 seasons, a lot of fingers were firmly pointed at Young.

When the 1992 season was about to begin, and Montana still wasn't ready to play, Coach George Seifert tapped Young as his starter, despite the fact that he had been outplayed by Bono in the preseason games. Although Young had gotten the nod from Seifert, he still had to win over the San Francisco fans and his own teammates, many of whom thought Bono was a better quarterback. Young also had to deal with the pressure of playing while Montana, a living legend, was waiting in the wings to reclaim his starter's role. But Young was also determined to seize his opportunity. "I'm here now, and it's my job."

Young took a giant step toward winning the confidence of his teammates when, in the 10th game of the season, he threw two fourth quarter touchdown passes to rally the 49ers to a 21–20 win over New Orleans and break a first-place tie with the Saints. "Those last drives, he was just as calm as Joe ever was," said veteran guard Joe McIntyre.

Young went on to gain even more trust as he led the 49ers to a 14–2 record, best in the NFL. Young, who was named the league's MVP, also repeated as the NFL's top-rated passer, while also leading the league in touchdown passes and completion percentage. "Now, I can't wait, I just can't wait for next season."

Born: October 11, 1961, in Salt Lake City, Utah
Height: 6′2″ Weight: 200
College: Brigham Young University
Round Drafted: First, in supplemental draft
NFL Seasons Played: 8

NFL CAREER STATS

ATT.	*COMP.*	*YDS.*	*TD'S*	*INT.*
1,506	908	11,877	76	42

ERIC ALLEN

DEFENSIVE BACK

PHILADELPHIA EAGLES

ERIC ALLEN
PHILADELPHIA EAGLES

Eric Allen has wanted to be a pro football player for as long as he can remember. "I love playing football, and I love being around the guys. This is what I've wanted to do my whole life."

Allen took his first step toward his goal when he earned all-county honors as a cornerback and running back at Point Loma High School in San Diego. In his senior season at Point Loma, Allen not only rushed for 909 yards, a 9-yard per carry average, he also returned four interceptions for touchdowns.

Then Allen moved on to Arizona State University, where he became a four-year starter at defensive back for the Sun Devils. Allen won honorable mention All-Pac-10 honors as a junior, and picked off a pass that helped ASU beat Michigan in the 1987 Rose Bowl, 22–15. In his senior season, Allen graduated to the first-team All-Pac 10 after he snatched eight passes and returned two of them for touchdowns, including a 92-yard romp against Washington State.

Allen showed so much talent during his four years at ASU that Buddy Ryan, the Philadelphia Eagles coach at the time, penciled Allen in as the starting right corner on the day that he drafted him. Allen quickly validated Ryan's judgment by picking off five passes, including four inside the Eagles' 20-yard line, on his way to winning NFL All-Rookie honors in 1988.

Only one year later, Allen upped his theft count to eight, tops in the NFC, and knocked down a team-high 25 passes, while earning All-Pro honors as well as his first trip to the Pro Bowl.

"Eric is the best cornerback I've ever been around as a player or a coach," says current Eagles coach Rich Kotite. "He does everything well. It's a comfort to see him out there because it doesn't matter who he's playing against, Eric is going to win more battles than he loses. His is the toughest position to play in terms of being out there all alone on the corner, but Eric does the job game after game. He's intelligent, he prepares himself, he's truly a complete player. There's nobody better; maybe two or three guys as good, but none better."

Although Allen has gone on to become a perennial Pro Bowl performer, and ranks right up at the top of the cornerback ratings along with Rod Woodson of the Pittsburgh Steelers and Washington's Darrell Green, Allen loves the game too much to take his status for granted. "I don't take it from season to season, I take it from week to week. It's nice to know that I'm regarded as one of the best cornerbacks in the game, but all I'm concerned with is whether I played that way last week and how I'm going to do this week. Am I still going to be one of the top one or two this week?"

Born: November 22, 1965, in San Diego, California
Height: 5′10″ Weight: 188
College: Arizona State
NFL Seasons Played: 5

CAREER STATS

TACKLES	*INT.*	*RETURN YARDS*	*TD'S*
287	25	49	0

EMMITT SMITH

RUNNING BACK

DALLAS COWBOYS

EMMITT SMITH
DALLAS COWBOYS

Although Emmitt Smith had been the prep school Player of the Year at Escambia High School in Pensacola, Florida, and had then gone on to become an All-American at the University of Florida where he set 58 school records, there were a lot of pro scouts who questioned his ability to become an impact player in the NFL.

Smith, though, put those doubts to rest with a sensational rookie season. Despite getting off to a slow start because of missing training camp and the preseason games, Smith rushed for 937 yards and 11 touchdowns to win the 1990 NFL Offensive Rookie of the Year award while being named to the NFC Pro Bowl squad.

The following year, Smith turned in a spectacular sophomore season, as he led the league in rushing, while becoming the 28th and youngest NFL player to go over 1,500 yards rushing in a season. Smith, who was the league's leading workhorse with 365 carries, piled up big pieces of his yardage against some of the NFL's top-rated defenses. Smith was the only runner to gain 100 yards rushing against the New Orleans Saints, who ranked second in the league in rushing defense. And he cracked the century mark twice against Washington, the only two times that the Super Bowl champions yielded 100 yards to a runner during the 1991 season. Smith continued to impress in the Cowboys' playoff game with Chicago, as he rumbled for 105 yards to become the first running back to ever gain 100 rushing yards against the Bears in postseason play, a record that spanned 27 games and dated back to 1932. "There's no question," said quarterback Troy Aikman, "our success is based on Emmitt running the ball."

While 1991 had appeared to be a signature season for Smith, he was even better in 1992. Smith shot right out of the blocks, stinging Washington in the season opener for 140 yards on the ground while earning the NFC Offensive Player of the Week award. Smith earned his second Player of the Week award in October against the Raiders, when he rambled for 152 yards and scored twice on the ground and once through the air. Two weeks later, Smith broke through for 163 yards against a top-rated Philadelphia Eagles defense that hadn't allowed a running back to crack the century mark in 53 straight games.

Smith, who was also named the NFC Offensive Player of the Month for November and December, closed out the season by racking up 131 yards against the Bears to earn his third Player of the Week award. That effort also allowed Smith to overtake Barry Foster and become only the ninth NFL player, and the first since Eric Dickerson in 1983–84, to win back-to-back rushing titles. He also became the first player to amass 1,500 rushing yards in consecutive seasons since Walter Payton, the NFL's all-time leading rusher, turned the trick in 1984–85.

Then Smith, who was the league's top touchdown-maker with 19, put the finishing touches on his scintillating season by rushing for over 100 yards in three straight postseason games, including Super Bowl XXVII. "I can't think of what would happen to our offense," said Cowboys coach Jimmy Johnson, "without Emmitt Smith."

Born: May 15, 1969, in Pensacola, Florida
Height: 5′9″ Weight: 209
College: University of Florida
Round Drafted: First
NFL Seasons Played: 3

CAREER STATS

RUSH		RECEPTS.		
YDS.	*AVG.*	*NO.*	*YDS.*	*TD'S*
4213	4.3	132	821	43

THURMAN THOMAS

RUNNING BACK

BUFFALO BILLS

THURMAN THOMAS
BUFFALO BILLS

As a ball player, Thurman Thomas has always had a chip on his shoulder. When he was younger, it was because he was the smallest boy in the neighborhood, and usually the last one to get picked when sides were chosen. "I thought, 'The heck with them.' When I'm challenged, I can do anything," said Thomas, who went on to become an all-state running back and lead Willowridge High School to an undefeated season and the 1982 class 4A Texas state championship.

The college coaches in the Southwest Conference, however, thought that Thomas was too small to play running back, so he wound up at Oklahoma State University. Thomas, though, showed how big he could play by racking up 1,650 yards in his sophomore season. After a serious offseason knee injury limited Thomas to 741 yards in his junior year, he snapped right back in his senior season by rushing for 1,613 yards, including an OSU-record 293 yards in the regular season finale. Then Thomas capped off his collegiate career with a record-setting four-touchdown eruption in the Sun Bowl.

With those credentials, Thomas looked like a sure-shot first round draft choice, and ESPN set up cameras in Thomas' apartment to record the magic moment. But what the cameras caught, instead, was Thomas' embarrassment as NFL teams, scared off by his surgical knee, allowed him to slip into the second round. As one veteran talent scout put it, "Buffalo got a first round back who has a last round knee."

But instead of burning his copy of the tape, Thomas has used it as a motivational device to fuel his NFL career. "I watch it all the time," said Thomas, whose career has become an unending series of highlight tapes.

Thomas, who was the NFL's Most Valuable Player in 1991, is not only a great runner, but he is also the game's most gifted and dangerous receiver coming out of the backfield. "I don't know if there's ever been a more complete back to play the game," said Bills head coach Marv Levy. "Here's a guy who can run, he can catch, he's very smart, and very competitive. He's a rare one."

Thomas showed just how special he was when in 1992 he became the first player in NFL history to lead the league in total yards from scrimmage for four consecutive years, breaking the record of three straight years that had been set by the legendary Jim Brown.

"Thomas could be the best player I've ever seen," said veteran wide receiver James Lofton. "He's as good as they come," added New England Patriots coach Bill Parcells. "He's in a class with Barry Sanders, but he catches the ball better. He can play on my team anytime."

Born: May 16, 1966, in Houston, Texas
Height: 5′10″ Weight: 198
College: Oklahoma State University
Round Drafted: Second
Seasons Played: 5

CAREER STATS

RUSH		*RECEPTS.*		
YDS.	*AVG.*	*NO.*	*YDS.*	*TD'S*
6,316	4.6	247	2,666	50

DAN MARINO

QUARTERBACK
MIAMI DOLPHINS

DAN MARINO
MIAMI DOLPHINS

Dan Marino has been rewriting the record book ever since he entered the league in 1983. Although young quarterbacks usually warm the bench for a few years, Marino not only started in his rookie season for the Dolphins, he starred.

Marino took over the reigns in the sixth game of the season and battered the Buffalo Bills for 322 yards and three touchdown tosses. And even though Miami lost the game in overtime, 38–35, Dolphin coach Don Shula knew that he had found a special player. "He has a toughness about him, a real desire to win. Even after he throws an interception, he comes out gunning. He's a winner because he's not afraid to lose."

Marino, who won the *Sporting News* Rookie of the Year award, wound up leading the AFC with a 96.0 passing rating, and became the only rookie to ever start a Pro Bowl game. But that fabulous freshman year was only a warm-up for the most remarkable season that any quarterback has ever had.

Marino came out smoking right from the git-go, wiping out Washington with five scoring strikes in the opening game of the 1984 season. And by the end of that singular season, Marino had shattered the all-time single-season record for touchdown passes with 48 (the previous NFL record had been 36), and had also set new standards for completions, with 362, and passing yardage, with 5,084. Marino, though, wasn't finished. He went on to sting the Seattle Seahawks on two scoring tosses in an opening-round playoff game, and set AFC Championship Game records by throwing for 421 yards and four touchdowns against the Pittsburgh Steelers. And even a Dolphin loss to a Joe-Montana-led San Francisco 49ers team in Super Bowl XIX couldn't diminish Marino's awesome accomplishments. "I find myself comparing him to John Unitas," said Shula, speaking of the Hall of Fame quarterback that he had coached in Baltimore. "And I didn't think I'd do that with any quarterback, much less a second-year one. Dan makes such quick decisions, has great peripheral vision, and the quickest arm I've ever seen. It's just boom, and the ball is gone."

Marino has continued to rewrite the NFL record book during the course of his first 10 years in the league. He is already the only quarterback in league history to pass for more than 4,000 yards in four different seasons, and he has reached the 30,000-yards-passed plateau and the 200-touchdown-passes-thrown mark faster than any other signal caller in the history of the game.

Marino has eclipsed all of his contemporaries in the major career categories, and now only trails a few Hall of Famers, mainly Unitas and Fran Tarkenton, both of whom put in 18 seasons in the league. With his durability—he's played in 140 straight games—Marino looks like a sure bet to finish his career at the top of most of the major quarterback rankings. Don Shula, for one, has absolutely no doubts. "He's going to break all the records in the book."

Born: September 15, 1961, in Pittsburgh, Pennsylvania
Height: 6′4″ Weight: 225
College: University of Pittsburgh
Round Drafted: First
NFL Seasons Played: 10

CARERR STATS

ATT.	*COMP.*	*YDS.*	*TD'S*	*INT.*
5,284	3,128	39,502	290	165

JUNIOR SEAU

LINEBACKER

SAN DIEGO CHARGERS

JUNIOR SEAU
SAN DIEGO CHARGERS

Junior Seau has been dazzling the fans in Southern California with his athleticism ever since he was a three-sport star at Ocean Side High School in San Diego. Although Seau was a gifted shot putter and the San Diego Section Basketball Player of the Year at Ocean Side, he made his major mark as a two-way football player, earning All-American honors as a senior for his linebacking play while also being named the Avocado League's Offensive Player of the Year as a tight end.

Seau then moved up the California coast to Los Angeles, where he carved out an All-American career for himself as an outside linebacker by recording 19 sacks and making 27 tackles behind the line of scrimmage in his junior year at USC. Three years after he had left, Seau made the return trip to San Diego after the Chargers made him the fifth choice in the 1990 NFL draft. "The Junior Seau's aren't hard to scout," said San Diego general manager Bobby Beathard. "The coach doesn't tell you, 'Look at the Cal game' or 'Look at the Oregon game.' They just tell you to pick anything, because he's always gaining at the same speed. He has the chance to be one of the real top ones ever at his position."

Although Seau had a fine rookie year, he was unhappy with being forced to move to the middle linebacker position. "I didn't know anything but outside linebacker," said Seau, who had always been a pass rusher. "All I knew was the blitz." But an off-season talk with a San Diego coach convinced Seau into believing that he could become one of the all-time great middle linebackers. "They showed they believed in me," said Seau. "So I decided to play the middle with a smile."

Seau also played the position with an intensity that made him the team's leading tackler and its second leading sacker while earning Seau All-AFC honors and his first Pro Bowl appearance. "They talk about Lawrence Taylor and Mike Singletary, but he's like both of them put into one," said Greg Townsend of the Los Angeles Raiders.

Seau was even better in 1992, as he spearheaded the Chargers to the top of the AFC's Western Division, which put them into the playoff picture for the first time in 10 year. "Junior Seau is the best defensive player we've faced, by a pretty good margin," said Cleveland coach Bill Belichick. "He does it all. He can play at the point of attack, he chases down plays, he plays the run, he plays the pass. Nobody's been able to stop him."

Even in the Chargers' 31–0 playoff loss to the Miami Dolphins, Seau, who registered 18 solo tackles and one assist, was simply awesome. "I'm glad," said Dolphins tight end Keith Jackson, who had seen enough of Seau, "that I'm on his team in the Pro Bowl."

Born: January 19, 1969, in San Diego, California
Height: 6′3″ Weight: 250
College: USC
Round Drafted: First
NFL Seasons Played: 3

CAREER STATS

		FUMBLES		
TACKLES	*SACKS*	*FORCED*	*RECOVERED*	*INT.*
320	12.5	1	1	2

JIM KELLY

QUARTERBACK

BUFFALO BILLS

JIM KELLY
BUFFALO BILLS

Jim Kelly showed that he might be something special as a football player when, as a 10-year-old, he was a national semifinalist in the Punt, Pass and Kick competition that the NFL used to help sponsor.

Kelly stayed with the sport, and in his senior season at East Bradley High School in Pittsburgh, Pennsylvania, he won all-state honors for linebacking as well as his quarterback play. He was such a promising linebacker that Penn State's head coach, Joe Paterno, who is known for sending top-flight linebackers into the NFL, offered Kelly a scholarship. Kelly, though, decided that he would rather play quarterback, so he instead accepted a scholarship to the University of Miami. "Actually, I much preferred being a linebacker. I don't like getting hit. I liked handing out the hits. But I liked being in control even more, so I decided to stick with quarterbacking."

During his four years at Miami, Kelly helped the Hurricanes to become a football powerhouse, and he also started a tradition of excellence at the quarterback position that has been continued by the likes of Bernie Kosar, Vinny Testaverde, Steve Walsh, and Gino Torretta, the 1992 Heisman Trophy winner. Kelly finished his junior season as one of the top quarterbacks in college football, while being named the ABC-TV Offensive Player of the Game three times, including one in which he led the Hurricanes to a 14–7 win over Penn State.

Although a shoulder injury caused Kelly to miss most of his senior season, he had already shown so much ability that the Bills passed up Dan Marino to make him their number one pick in the 1983 draft. Kelly, though, decided to pass on the NFL and sign with the Houston Gamblers of the rival United States Football League.

Kelly took to the Gamblers' run-and-shoot offense as if he'd been born playing it. In his first season in Houston he threw for 5,219 yards and 44 touchdowns while winning the league's MVP award. During his two-year stint with the Gamblers, Kelly threw for 9,842 yards and 83 touchdowns—big numbers in any league—while twice being named All-USFL.

Kelly finally joined the Bills in 1986, and two years later he was named to the Pro Bowl after leading Buffalo to the top spot in the AFC's Eastern Division. Over the last three seasons, Kelly has helped turn the Bills' fast-break-style no-huddle offense into one of the NFL's top scoring units, while leading Buffalo to three straight Super Bowl appearances. And while some critics point a finger at Kelly for not bringing the Vince Lombardi Trophy home to Buffalo, there are others who suggest that that makes as much sense as knocking someone for winning a silver medal in the Olympic Games. "We've made it three times," said Kelly. "There's a lot of teams that have never made it to the Big Dance."

And the reason that those teams haven't made it to the Super Bowl, according to Steve Tasker, the Bills' Pro Bowl special teams player, is simple. "They don't have Jim Kelly."

Born: February 14, 1960, in Pittsburgh, Pennsylvania
Height: 6′3″ Weight: 218
College: University of Miami
Round Drafted: First
NFL Seasons Played: 7

NFL CAREER STATS

ATT.	*COMP.*	*YDS.*	*TD'S*	*INT.*
3,024	1,824	23,031	161	108

BARRY FOSTER

RUNNING BACK

PITTSBURGH STEELERS

BARRY FOSTER
PITTSBURGH STEELERS

Barry Foster started establishing himself as a top-notch football player at Duncanville High School in Texas, where he earned all-state honors after rushing for more than 1,500 yards in his senior season. "Football kept me out of trouble, kept me out of the streets and kept me from running with the wrong crowds. It kept me focused and clear of danger."

Foster then went on to the University of Arkansas, where he had a solid but unspectacular career, finishing his three-year stint as the sixth leading rusher in Razorback history. He left school after his junior year to play for pay in the NFL because he wanted to help support his mother, Sharon, who had become disabled.

The pro scouts, though, didn't see a bright future for Foster in the NFL, so he languished until the fifth round of the 1990 draft, when he was finally taken by the Pittsburgh Steelers after 127 other players, including 18 running backs, had already been selected.

Foster was used sparingly in his rookie year, never getting more than six rushes in a game, until the next-to-last contest when he toted the pigskin 16 times and rushed for 100 yards. The following year, Foster gained 428 yards in his first seven games and seemed headed for a possible 1,000-yard season until an ankle injury sidelined him for six of the team's final nine games. Although he had the ability to play in the NFL, nothing that Foster had done during his first two seasons in the league prepared anyone for what he was about to accomplish throughout the 1992 season. In fact, Foster sat out part of training camp in a contract dispute, and didn't even know if he would be the Steelers' starting running back. "I didn't know *what* role I was going to play."

Foster, though, won the starting job and then began the season with a bang by rushing for 107 yards against the Houston Oilers. A week later he exploded for 190 yards and two touchdowns, including a 54-yard scoring gallop, against the New York Jets. And the fireworks kept bursting week after week as Foster rushed for more than 100 yards in 12 diffeent games, tying a record established by Eric Dickerson in 1984 while he was playing for the Los Angeles Rams. Foster, who shattered five of the single-season Steeler rushing records that had been set by Hall of Famer Franco Harris, wound up as the AFC's leading rusher with 1,690 yards, only 23 behind NFL-leading Emmitt Smith. "He accelerates into the line of scrimmage better than any back in the league," declared Buffalo Bills coach Marv Levy. "When he sees the hole, he explodes into it. He can cut on a dime and really get up the field."

And now, Barry Foster, the running back that no one really wanted, has become a Pro Bowl starter and the AFC Player of the Year.

Born: December 8, 1968, in Hurst, Texas
Height: 5′10″ Weight: 214
College: University of Arkansas
Round Drafted: Fifth
NFL Seasons Played: 3

CAREER STATS

RUSH		*RECEPTS.*		
YDS.	*AVG.*	*NO.*	*YDS.*	*TD'S*
2381	4.6	46	463	13

JOHN ELWAY

QUARTERBACK
DENVER BRONCOS

JOHN ELWAY
DENVER BRONCOS

The college class of 1983, which included running back Eric Dickerson and quarterbacks Dan Marino and Jim Kelly, produced what is generally considered to be the finest group of football players ever drafted by the NFL. But the one player that was at the top of every team's list was John Elway.

"There's probably never been anyone who's ever had a greater impact on the game of college football," said veteran coach Darryl Rogers. "He may be the best quarterback in the history of NCAA football."

Elway, who set five major passing records as a three-year starter at Stanford University, has also gone on to establish himself as one of the best all-time signal callers in the NFL. During his 10-year career with the Denver Broncos, Elway has led the team to six playoff berths, five AFC Western Division titles, and three victories in four AFC Championship Games. While critics point to Elway's 0–3 record in Super Bowl games, the reality is that those Denver teams only made it to the Big Game because of Elway's powerful arm and quick feet. "He carried the Broncos to those Super Bowls by his own sheer athletic ability," said 49ers offensive coordinator Mike Shanahan. "There hasn't been another quarterback in the NFL—now or in the past 30 years—who could have gotten those Denver teams into the Super Bowl."

Elway, who is the only quarterback in the history of the league to pass for over 3,000 yards and rush for over 200 yards in seven straight seasons, also has an amazing ability to turn losing games into victories. Like a magician, Elway has engineered 31 fourth-quarter, game-saving drives for the Broncos during regular season play.

Elway also showed that he could pull a win out of his helmet in a championship game when he directed Denver to a 23–20 overtime win over the Cleveland Browns in the 1986 title contest, one of the greatest comebacks in postseason history. First, Elway drove the Broncos 98 yards to the tying touchdown with only 39 seconds left in regulation time, a feat that has entered football lore as "The Drive." Then Elway led the Broncos on a 60-yard march in the overtime period that positioned Rich Karlis' game-winning field goal. "When you've got No. 7, anything is possible," said former Denver coach Dan Reeves. "The guy is unbelievable."

Six years later, Elway made believers out of the Houston Oilers by putting up 10 points in the last few minutes of a divisional playoff game. "He's amazing," said Gary Kubiak, Elway's backup at the time. "There are a lot of teams around the league who have had their hearts broken by John Elway in the last two minutes. We're just lucky to have him on our side."

"There's no other quarterback you would want in that situation," said Roger Staubach, the Hall of Fame quarterback who led Dallas to 23 fourth-quarter comebacks. "He beats you when you think you have him under control. But you never do have him under control. And that's the reason there's no quarterback in the game today that is more feared than John Elway."

Born: June 28, 1960, in Port Angeles, Washington
Height: 6′3″ Weight: 215
College: Stanford
Round Drafted: First
NFL Seasons Played: 10

CAREER STATS

ATT.	*COMP.*	*YDS.*	*TD'S*	*INT.*
4,339	2,375	30,216	156	157

CORTEZ KENNEDY

DEFENSIVE TACKLE

SEATTLE SEAHAWKS

CORTEZ KENNEDY
SEATTLE SEAHAWKS

Until the summer before Cortez Kennedy's senior season at the University of Miami, his so-far mediocre athletic career seemed to be headed for a close. Kennedy appeared resigned and content to be an underachieving, overweight backup defensive tackle without any pro prospects. He had so little drive and stamina that his Hurricane teammates nicknamed him Two-Play Tez. "He'd kill you for two plays, then take the next 20 off," said Randy Shamon, a Miami coach.

Coaches and teammates, including Russell Maryland, now with the Dallas Cowboys, tried to motivate Kennedy and help him kick his overeating habit. "If I could lose weight, he could lose weight," declared Maryland, who had dropped over 40 pounds and turned himself into an All-American lineman. But the person who finally got Kennedy to cut the calories and get to work was the late Jerome Brown, a former All-American for the Hurricanes who had gone on to become a Pro Bowl defensive tackle for the Philadelphia Eagles. Brown decided to take Kennedy under his extra-large wing, and the two men, who became best friends, spent the summer working out and watching films of Brown in action so that Kennedy could study the techniques that had made Brown so successful.

The program worked so well that Kennedy turned into a 285-pound tiger who earned All-American honors for himself, while helping Miami become the No. 1 team in the nation. "I've never seen a college football player have more impact on a game than Cortez," said the Hurricanes coach, Dennis Erickson. "No player in the country did more than he did last season. He created so many problems with his penetration. Once he set his mind to controlling his weight, he became a great player."

Kennedy's stock had risen so high that the Seattle Seahawks traded two No. 1 draft picks to the New England Patriots to ensure that they could snare him with the third pick of the 1990 NFL draft. Kennedy paid off immediate dividends for the Seahawks by earning All-Rookie honors before graduating to the Pro Bowl in 1991.

Then, in June of 1992, tragedy intruded on Kennedy's life when Jerome Brown and his 12-year-old nephew were killed in an automobile accident. "I cried all night," said Kennedy. "At first I didn't know how I could play again. But then I realized that I've got to be strong, because I'm a big factor on this team."

Kennedy decided to show his respect and affection for Brown by dedicating the 1992 season to his friend and wearing number 99, the number that Brown had worn with the Eagles. Then Kennedy, who runs with linebacker-like speed despire packing 293 pounds on his 6′3″ body, turned in a season-long display of highlight-film-type plays that earned him the NFL Defensive Player of the Year Award.

Kennedy, who remembers what it was like to be mediocre, is modest about his success. "I don't consider myself a superstar. I just work hard every day to get better, but I won't ever take myself or my accomplishments too seriously."

Born: August 23, 1968, in Wilson, Arkansas
Height: 6′3″ Weight: 293
College: University of Miami
Round Drafted: First
NFL Seasons Played: 3

CAREER STATS

		FUMBLES	
TACKLES	*SACKS*	*FORCED*	*RECOVERED*
213	21.5	6	3

WARREN MOON

QUARTERBACK

HOUSTON OILERS

WARREN MOON
HOUSTON OILERS

Warren Moon has wanted to be an NFL star ever since he put on the pads in a Pop Warner league as a 10-year-old. "When I was a kid, I used to dream about being a pro football player. I mean, I loved football. Even when I took out the trash, I'd run across the grass pretending I was O.J. Simpson, who was playing college ball at USC."

But Moon had to travel a hard and bumpy road before he could turn his boyhood dream into a reality. "He's worked hard for everything he's gotten, from the time he was a little boy," said Moon's mom, who made sure he did his homework and his share of household chores. "He was determined to accomplish his goals."

Although Moon didn't crack the Hamilton High School starting lineup until his final year, his senior season was so spectacular that he was named the MVP of the city of Los Angeles as well as a prep school All-American. But the big-time college recruiters didn't think that Moon had the goods to play quarterback at that level, so Moon wound up at West Los Angeles Junior College. "UCLA was the school I really wanted to play for, but they kept telling me that they wanted me to play another position."

But after watching Moon produce a record-setting freshman season at West LA, the University of Washington came through with a scholarship. Three years later Moon rewarded that decision by putting on an MVP performance while guiding the Huskies to a 27–20 win over Michigan in the 1978 Rose Bowl.

Because Moon knew that NFL teams didn't think too highly of his capabilities, he signed to play with Edmonton in the Canadian Football League. In his six seasons in the CFL, Moon led the Eskimos to the Grey Cup championship (the CFL version of the Super Bowl) five straight times, while throwing for over 5,000 yards in each of his final two seasons, including an all-time pro football record 5,648 yards in 1983. Although Moon, the CFL's MVP in 1983, had loved playing in Canada, he decided to accept a contract from the Houston Oilers, one of seven NFL teams that had beat a path to his door. "There was still something burning inside of me everytime I watched an NFL game—something that said, 'I can play with these guys.' It was time for me to prove just how good a quarterback I was."

Moon stepped right into a starting roll with the Oilers, a team that had lost 54 of its previous 66 games, and threw for over 3,000 yards while earning All-NFL Rookie honors in 1984. And within three seasons, his talent and leadership helped transform a sorry squad into a playoff team.

Moon has gone on to lead the Oilers into the playoffs in each of the last six seasons, while becoming only the second quarterback in NFL history to throw for more than 4,000 yards in consecutive seasons. In 1991, Moon, who seems to get better with age, set an NFL record for completions, with 404, and attempts, with 653. And in 1992 Moon, who has made the Pro Bowl for five straight seasons, became pro football's all-time passing leader with 51, 428 yards, including the yardage amassed in the CFL. "He's in a class by himself," declared Oilers general manager Mike Holovak.

Born: November 18, 1956, in Los Angeles, California
Height: 6′3″ Weight: 212
College: University of Washington
Round Drafted: Signed as a free agent
NFL Seasons Played: 9

NFL CAREER STATS

ATT.	*COMP.*	*YDS.*	*TD'S*	*INT.*
4,026	2,329	30,200	175	145

A.F.C. LEADERS

QUARTERBACKS

	Att	Comp	Pct Comp	Yds	Gain	TD	Int	Rating Points
Moon, Warren, Hou.	346	224	64.7	2521	7.29	18	12	89.3
Marino, Dan, Mia.	554	330	59.6	4116	7.43	24	16	85.1
O'Donnell, Neil, Pit.	313	185	59.1	2283	7.29	13	9	83.6
Kelly, Jim, Buf.	462	269	58.2	3457	7.48	23	19	81.2
Carlson, Cody, Hou.	227	149	65.6	1710	7.53	9	11	81.2
Krieg, Dave, K.C.	413	230	55.7	3115	7.54	15	12	79.9
Humphries, Stan, S.D.	454	263	57.9	3356	7.39	16	18	76.4
Elway, John, Den.	316	174	55.1	2242	7.09	10	17	65.7
Schroeder, Jay, Rai.	253	123	48.6	1476	5.83	11	11	63.3
George, Jeff, Ind.	306	167	54.6	1963	6.42	7	15	61.5
Esiason, Boomer, Cin.	278	144	51.8	1407	5.06	11	15	57.0
Nagle, Browning, NY-J	387	192	49.6	2280	5.89	7	17	55.7
Gelbaugh, Stan, Sea.	255	121	47.5	1307	5.13	6	11	52.9

RUSHERS

	Att	Yards	Avg	Long	TD
Foster, Barry, Pit.	390	1690	4.3	69	11
Thomas, Thurman, Buf.	312	1487	4.8	44	9
White, Lorenzo, Hou.	265	1226	4.6	44	7
Green, Harold, Cin.	265	1170	4.4	53	2
Warren, Chris, Sea.	223	1017	4.6	52	3
Higgs, Mark, Mia.	256	915	3.6	23	7
Butts, Marion, S.D.	218	809	3.7	22	4
Dickerson, Eric, Rai.	187	729	3.9	40t	2
Baxter, Brad, NY-J	152	698	4.6	30	6
Green, Gaston, Den.	161	648	4.0	67t	2
Davis, Kenneth, Buf.	139	613	4.4	64t	6
Word, Barry, K.C.	163	607	3.7	44t	4
Johnson, Anthony, Ind.	178	592	3.3	19	0

RECEIVERS

	No	Yards	Avg	Long	TD
Jeffires, Haywood, Hou.	90	913	10.1	47	9
Duncan, Curtis, Hou.	82	954	11.6	72	1
Harmon, Ronnie, S.D.	79	914	11.6	55	1
Williams, John L., Sea.	74	556	7.5	27	2
Miller, Anthony, S.D.	72	1060	14.7	67t	7
Givins, Earnest, Hou.	67	787	11.7	41	10
Reed, Andre, Buf.	65	913	14.0	51	3
Langhorne, Reggie, Ind.	65	811	12.5	34	1
Thomas, Thurman, Buf.	58	626	10.8	43	3
Burkett, Chris, NY-J	57	724	12.7	37t	1
White, Lorenzo, Hou.	57	641	11.2	69t	1
Fryar, Irving, N.E.	55	791	14.4	54t	4
Humphrey, Bobby, Mia.	54	507	9.4	26	1

PUNTERS

	No	Yards	Avg	Long	Total Punts
Montgomery, Greg, Hou.	53	2487	46.9	66	55
Stark, Rohn, Ind.	83	3716	44.8	64	83
Tuten, Rick, Sea.	108	4760	44.1	65	108
Barker, Bryan, K.C.	75	3245	43.3	65	76
Royals, Mar, Pit.	73	3119	42.7	58	74
Kidd, John, S.D.	68	2899	42.6	65	68
Gossett, Jeff, Rai.	77	3255	42.3	56	77
Mohr, Chris, Buf.	60	2531	42.2	61	60
Johnson, Lee, Cin.	76	3196	42.1	64	76
Hansen, Brian, Cle.	74	3083	41.7	73	75
McCarthy, Shawn, N.E.	103	4227	41.0	61	103
Aguiar, Louie, NY-J	73	2993	41.0	65	73

PUNT RETURNERS

	No	FC	Yards	Avg	Long	TD
Woodson, Rod, Pit.	32	13	364	11.4	80t	1
Verdin, Clarence, Ind.	24	12	268	11.2	84t	2
Marshall, Arthur, Den.	33	16	349	10.6	47	0
Carter, Dale, K.C.	38	6	398	10.5	86t	2
Brown, Tim, Rai.	37	6	398	10.4	40	0
Hicks, Cliff, Buf.	29	6	289	10.0	42	0
Metcalf, Eric, Cle.	44	10	429	9.8	75t	1
Stanley, Walter, N.E.	28	17	227	8.1	50	1
Bieniemy, Eric, S.D.	30	3	229	7.6	21	0
Carpenter, Rob, NY-J	28	9	208	7.4	21	0
Warren, Chris, Sea.	34	25	252	7.4	16	0

KICKOFF RETURNERS

	No	Yards	Avg	Long	TD
Vaughn, Jon, N.E.	20	564	28.2	100t	1
Baldwin, Randy, Cle.	30	675	22.5	47	0
Montgomery, Alton, Den.	21	466	22.2	64	0
Verdin, Clarence, Ind.	39	815	20.9	42	0
Ball, Eric, Cin.	20	411	20.6	48	0
Williams, Harvey, K.C.	21	405	19.3	37	0
McMillan, Erik, NY-J	22	420	19.1	45	0
Woodson, Rod, Pit.	25	469	18.8	32	0
Warren, Chris, Sea.	28	524	18.7	34	0
Stanley, Walter, N.E.	29	529	18.2	40	0
Mathis, Terance, NY-J	28	492	17.6	32	0
Stegall, Milt, Cin.	25	430	17.2	39	0

TOUCHDOWN LEADERS

	TD	Rush	Rec	Misc.	Pts
Thomas, Thurman, Buf. . .	12	9	3	0	72
Foster, Barry, Pit.	11	11	0	0	66
Givins, Earnest, Hou. . . .	10	0	10	0	60
Culver, Rodney, Ind. . . .	9	7	2	0	54
Jeffires, Haywood, Hou.	9	0	9	0	54
Fenner, Derrick, Cin. . . .	8	7	1	0	48
Jackson, Mark, Den. . . .	8	0	8	0	48
Miller, Anthony, S.D. . . .	8	0	7	1	48
White, Lorenzo, Hou. . . .	8	7	1	0	48
Brown, Tim, Rai.	7	0	7	0	42
Duper, Mark, Mia.	7	0	8	0	42
Higgs, Mark, Mia.	7	7	0	0	42

KICKING

	EP	EPA	FG	FGA	PTS
Stoyanovich, Pete, Mia.	34	36	30	37	124
Christie, Steve, Buf.	43	44	24	30	115
Anderson, Gary, Pit.	29	31	28	36	115
Carney, John, S.D.	35	35	26	32	113
Lowery, Nick, K.C.	39	39	22	24	105
Del Greco, Al, Hou.	41	41	21	27	104
Stover, Matt, Cle.	29	30	21	29	92
Breech, Jim, Cin.	31	31	19	27	88
Treadwell, David, Den.	28	28	20	24	88

TEAM OFFENSE

	Rush Yds.	Pass Yds.	Tot. Yds.	Rush TD	Pass TD	Misc. TD	E.P.	F.G./F.G.A.	Points
Buffalo	2436	3457	5893	18	23	3	43	24/30	381
Houston	1626	4029	5655	10	27	4	41	21/27	352
Kansas City	1532	2792	4324	14	15	11	39	23/25	348
Miami	1525	3975	5500	9	24	3	34	30/37	340
San Diego	1875	3346	5221	18	16	2	35	26/32	335
Pittsburgh	2156	2750	4906	13	15	3	29	28/36	299
Cincinnati	1976	1943	3919	11	16	4	31	19/28	274
Cleveland	1607	2885	4492	7	18	5	29	21/29	272
Denver	1500	2930	4430	11	16	2	28	20/25	262
L.A. Raiders	1794	2590	4384	7	20	2	28	15/26	249
N.Y. Jets	1752	2679	4431	8	12	3	23	19/30	220
Indianapolis	1102	3266	4368	8	13	3	24	16/29	216
New England	1550	2034	3584	6	13	6	22	11/17	205
Seattle	1596	1778	3374	4	9	1	14	14/22	140

SACK LEADERS

O'Neal, Leslie, S.D. 17.0
Fletcher, Simon, Den. 16.0
Smith, Neil, K.C. 14.5
Thomas, Derrick, K.C. 14.5
Cox, Bryan, Mia. 14.0
Kennedy, Cortez, Sea. 14.0
Smith, Bruce, Buf. 14.0
Childress, Ray, Hou. 13.0
Smith, Anthony, Rai. 13.0
Williams, Lee, Hou. 11.0
Mims, Chris, S.D. 10.0
Williams, Alfred, Cin. 10.0
Porter, Rufus, Sea. 9.5

INTERCEPTION LEADERS

	No	Yards	Avg	Long	TD
Jones, Henry, Buf.	8	263	32.9	82t	2
Robinson, Eugene, Sea.	7	126	18.0	49	0
Carter, Dale, K.C.	7	65	9.3	36t	1
Kelso, Mar, Buf.	7	21	3.0	13	0
Carrington, Darren, S.D.	6	152	25.3	69	1
Brim, Michael, NY-J . . .	6	139	23.2	77t	1
Perry, Darren, Pit.	6	69	11.5	34	0
Washington, Brian, NY-J	6	59	9.8	23t	1
Prior, Mike, Ind.	6	44	7.3	19	0
Gray, Jerry, Hou.	6	24	4.0	22	0

TEAM DEFENSE

	Rush Yds.	Pass Yds.	Tot. Yds.	Opp. TD	Rush TD	Pass TD	Ret. TD	Sacks	Int.	Pts. Allow
Pittsburgh	1841	2817	4658	24	6	15	3	36	22	225
San Diego	1395	2832	4227	29	10	17	2	51	25	241
Houston	1634	2577	4211	28	6	20	2	50	20	258
Cleveland	1605	3152	4757	29	5	23	1	48	13	275
Raiders	1683	2833	4516	32	17	11	4	46	12	281
Miami	1600	2983	4583	32	9	16	7	36	18	281
Kansas City	1787	2537	4324	34	12	19	3	50	24	282
Buffalo	1395	3209	4604	31	8	19	4	44	23	283
Indianapolis	2174	2900	5074	34	16	14	4	39	20	303
Seattle	1922	2661	4583	32	14	11	7	46	20	312
NY Jets	1919	2961	4880	35	13	19	3	36	21	315
Denver	1963	3120	5083	35	10	21	4	50	15	329
New England	1951	3097	5048	40	15	22	3	20	14	363
Cincinnati	2007	3326	5333	44	15	24	5	45	16	364

PRO BOWL ROSTER
AMERICAN CONFERENCE

OFFENSE

WIDE RECEIVERS—Curtis Duncan, Oilers; Ernest Givins, Oilers; Andre Reed, Bills; Haywood Jeffires, Oilers; Anthony Miller, Chargers.
TIGHT ENDS—Marv Cook, Patroits; Shannon Sharpe, Broncos.
TACKLES—Richmond Webb, Dolphins; Howard Ballard, Bills; John Alt, Chiefs.
GUARDS—Jim Ritcher, Bills; Mike Munchak, Oilers; Carlton Haseirig, Steelers.
CENTERS—Dermontti Dawson, Steelers; Bruce Matthews, Oilers.
QUARTERBACKS—Warren Moon, Oilers; Dan Marino, Dolphins, Neil O'Donnell, Steelers.
RUNNING BACKS—Harold Green, Bengals; Barry Foster, Steelers; Ronnie Harmon, Chargers; Lorenzo White, Oilers.

DEFENSE

DEFENSIVE ENDS—Neil Smith, Chiefs; Leslie O'Neal, Chargers; Howie Long, Raiders.
NOSE TACKLES—Ray Childress, Oilers; Cortez Kennedy, Seahawks.
LINEBACKERS—Bryan Cox, Dolphins; Al Smith, Oilers; Junior Seau, Chargers; Michael Brooks, Broncos; Derrick Thomas, Chiefs; Greg Lloyd, Steelers; Cornelius Bennett, Bills.
CORNERBACKS—Rod Woodson, Steelers; Terry McDaniel, Raiders; Nate Odomes, Bills.
SAFETIES—Henry Jones, Bills; Steve Atwater, Broncos; Eugene Robinson, Seahawks.

SPECIALISTS

PUNTER—Rohn Stark, Colts.

PLACE-KICKER—Nick Lowery, Chiefs.

KICK RETURNER—Clarence Verdin, Colts.

SPECIAL TEAMS—Steve Tasker, Bills.

PREDICTIONS FOR THE 1993 SEASON

This year the crystal ball is particularly clouded because of the player movement brought about by free agency. It's difficult to predict how players will fit in with new teams, and how well teams are able to adjust to the loss of some top talent.

There's also been lots of changes in the coaching ranks, including: Dan Reeves coming over from the Denver Broncos to the New York Giants; Dave Wannstedt, the former defensive coordinator of the Dallas Cowboys, taking over the Chicago Bears from Mike Ditka and former Giants coach, Bill Parcells, who left the cozy confines of the television booth to take on the job of trying to revive the long-dormant New England Patriots.

But okay, I'm ready to throw the darts.

NATIONAL CONFERENCE

EAST	CENTRAL	WEST
Dallas	Green Bay	San Francisco
Washington	Detroit	New Orleans
Philadelphia	Minnesota	Atlanta
New York Giants	Chicago	LA Rams
Phoenix	Tampa Bay	

AMERICAN CONFERENCE

EAST	CENTRAL	WEST
Miami	Houston	Kansas City
Buffalo	Pittsburgh	San Diego
Indianapolis	Cleveland	LA Raiders
New York Jets	Cincinnati	Seattle
New England		

The Dallas Cowboys are the reigning Super Bowl Champions and they should top the NFC East again. The Central division figures to be a scramble among the top three teams, with the presence of ex-Eagle Reggie White giving the Packers a slight edge. The 49ers lost last years NFC championship game to Dallas and then they lost defensive end Pierce Holt to free agency, and traded Joe Montana. But they've retained enough talent to take the west.

In the AFC East, it's hard not to pick the Bills. But they were hurt by free agency and they might not be able to bounce back from their third successive Super Bowl loss. My head tells me that the Steelers should win the Central division, but my heart is with Warren Moon. In the West, Joe Montana, if he can stay healthy, will be the missing piece in Kansas City's puzzle. If not, look for the Chargers to take the top spot.

It's a long way from now to January, but I'll predict that the Dallas Cowboys will repeat as champions by defeating Kansas City in Super Bowl XXVIII—if Troy Aikman has enough time to recover from his back surgery. If he doesn't, I'll ride with the 49ers.

CHALLENGE THE EXPERT

I hope that you have an easier time making your picks than I did making mine.

NATIONAL CONFERENCE

EAST	CENTRAL	WEST
1. ____________	1. ____________	1. ____________
2. ____________	2. ____________	2. ____________
3. ____________	3. ____________	3. ____________
4. ____________	4. ____________	4. ____________
5. ____________	5. ____________	

NFC Champion: ____________

AMERICAN CONFERENCE

EAST	CENTRAL	WEST
1. ____________	1. ____________	1. ____________
2. ____________	2. ____________	2. ____________
3. ____________	3. ____________	3. ____________
4. ____________	4. ____________	4. ____________
5. ____________		5. ____________

AFC Champion: ____________

SUPER BOWL XXVIII Winner: ____________